Let's Write A Feature

By G. Thomas Duffy

SCHOOL OF JOURNALISM
UNIVERSITY OF MISSOURI

Lucas
Brothers
Publishers

909 LOWRY
COLUMBIA, MISSOURI 65201

Let's Write a Feature
Copyright 1969
G. Thomas Duffy

Library of Congress Catalog Card Number 74-94843

Standard Book Number 87543-056-2

Printed in the United States of America

Contents

PREFACE

I had two goals in mind when I decided, after six years in the academic field of Journalism and more than thirty years in the professional newspaper field, to write this book, "Let's Write a Feature!" One was to furnish the Journalism student with a primer-type text on feature writing. The other was to make that student comfortable as he learned to write a feature story.

This text was written with awareness of the growing importance of the feature writer, from newsfeatures through profiles to major interpretatives, in the world of Journalism today. It also was written with the feeling that far too many textbooks on the market today emphasize HOW TO SELL the feature story and de-emphasize HOW TO WRITE the feature story. It is my conviction that the student and, yes, the young reporter in the professional field, must learn HOW TO WRITE before he even thinks of HOW TO SELL.

In so doing, it also is my conviction that the student must be comfortable, at ease as he learns. Thus, my decision to abandon the NAME writers of the past and present as examples; to use as examples feature stories actually written by students in this course. It has been my experience in using this text as the basis for lectures in my classes that the decision is correct: Beginners are more at ease with beginners and the learning process becomes easier.

Chapter I

The Approach

This book is dedicated to you — the scared kid in the college classroom, the scared kid just breaking into professional journalism. You want to write well but you're terrified by the suggestion of an assignment outside the familiar, rigid format of the straight news story.

You tell yourself that you have had a tough time learning how to write the news story to the satisfaction of your instructors or editors. Now, either by choice or the will of your teacher or editor, you're assigned to a mysterious thing called a feature story. And you're told that if you want to succeed in journalism — whether in the newspaper, magazine, radio or television field — you must learn how to write that feature story.

What about the guys who spend their professional careers covering the police beat? You ask about that as you reflect upon the comfortable assignments to write straight news reports on drunks and holdups and traffic offenders or the college student covering campus news. Why can't a guy go on writing simple, little news reports all his life? Well, journalism has changed since your father and your grandfather broke into the game. Today's police reporter must interpret the news as well as report the daily record. He must be alert to the humorous side of life as well as the sordid, and he must be able to write about it. This is what journalism in all its aspects demands of the writer-reporter today.

Before you, in all fields of journalism, stand reporters who will assure you that feature writing is demanding but it is fun, it is educational, it's a key to advancement through its improvement of your reportorial skill and the bylines through which you earn professional attention.

You're not abandoning your original ambition to be a reporter; you're now beginning to learn how to be a FIRST-CLASS reporter in whatever field of journalism you may choose as a career.

With that in mind, let's push aside that "mystery" aspect of feature writing. There is nothing mysterious about it, unless you are bewildered by today's clamor over "depth reporting" and the suggestion that there no longer is such a thing as a feature story. Suppose we recoginze two points as we begin learning how to write a feature story: (1) Depth reporting is a grown-up offspring of feature writing; (2) you, as a beginner, will be reporting in depth long before you are assigned to do an interpretative, which is journalese for depth reporting. It was the trained feature writer who grabbed the early bylines when interpretative or depth reporting became popular. The feature writer, on a lesser and usually more humorous basis, had been reporting in depth years before publishers and editors recognized the need to explain the news as well as report it. For feature writing simply is the business of getting the story BEHIND the story and presenting that story in an easy, dramatic, entertaining fashion for the enlightenment and enjoyment of the reader.

Why do we say "easy?" Because more often than not your reader of the feature story is sitting in his easy chair, trying to relax after a long day of battling the job and reading depressing headlines hurriedly. He wants to read some more, but he wants to read in comfort. Purposely, he has delayed glancing at the in-depth reports and the more cheerful news in his newspaper or magazine until he could reach this stage of the day. He wants to be attracted to those reports and he shall be if your feature story has punch from the outset. He does not want to be forced to consult a dictionary for definition of words you use. He wants to be entertained and educated, if you as the feature writer can add to his education in candy-coated fashion whether you make him laugh or cry as he reads.

If you have accomplished this in your feature story –

whether it's a brightener, a newsfeature, a profile or an interpretative – you will have made more impact upon that reader than most any screaming headline he may have read or heard earlier. If you haven't hit the goal, the reader will have ceased reading your story long before your ending and your byline will be remembered only as a clue to avoid your stuff in the future.

There is, of course, a formula to aid you in hitting that goal. You might call them fundamental rules. I hesitate to mention them in a way. After all this talk about feature writing being fun and educational and a key to advancement and fame for the writer, I can imagine you muttering. "Ha, now comes the old classroom routine gimmick."

Well, yes the rules ARE a gimmick. They're a gimmick to master, as a beginner, so that as you acquire experience and develop your own style and skill you can BREAK THEM! All of the giants in the field break the rules but they are able to do so because they have mastered them at the beginning, have acquired the experience through constant application to break those rules skillfully.

For, you see, you learn to write by WRITING!

Feature writing is a business you learn as you would learn to become a football, tennis or swimming star: By constant practice.

This is the premise, then, upon which we shall tackle the feature story. It is a sound premise. The lecturer in the classroom or the editor may as well recite the Constitution backward for all the value lectures may have unless that instruction is geared to practical application.

It's that simple: You learn to write feature stories by WRITING feature stories. The editor and instructor helps you primarily by speedily editing your copy and pointing out your mistakes while the subject is fresh in your mind. You learn to write feature stories by revision, rewriting your stories again and again if necessary and if there is time. Usually there is time in the classroom. In the professional field if a deadline must be met the editor will assign your copy to a trained rewrite man for quick revision. Your cue, then, is to study the published product, consult your editor AFTER deadline as to where you failed.

Feature writing is a cooperative venture for the writer and editor. Without that cooperation nothing is gained; with it, there is everything to be gained.

Well, then: We have been discussing some of the philosophy behind this business of writing feature stories. Let's look at the story itself. Just what IS a feature story? For a starter, consider this example:

> The Governor's Committee on the Arts was told today that more leisure time for workers has resulted in more interest in the arts.

Can you imagine that reader in his easy chair and wanting to be entertained and/or educated in entertaining fashion EAGERLY reading the rest of this story?

But the student, assigned to do a feature story, wrote this lead:

> There are more painters in the United States than there are hunters.
>
> More persons play the piano than hold fishing licenses.
>
> Concerts and recitals attracted twice as many persons last year as did all major league baseball games.
>
> And the Empire State Building is the only place attracting more servicemen on leave in New York than the Museum of Modern Art.

See the difference? Your reader in the easy chair may not be an artist, but it's almost a cinch that he either is a hunter, a fisherman, a baseball fan, an ex-serviceman— or all of them. And whether he's expressing amazement or simply sneering, he's reading that story!

The story behind the story. Told with a PUNCH calculated to intrigue the reader from the first word.

It's the story behind that meek little man you see trudging off to work at 7 a.m. and trudging home from work at 7 p.m. day after day after day. It's the story behind the routine obituary notice your undertaker drones through the phone. It's the story behind the ditchdigger or the construction worker or the "sidewalk superintendent." It's the explanation, in understandable language, of the story behind the headline on Vietnam or an ecumenical council at the Vatican. It's the story of the girl who lost her shoe down a manhole as she walked across the street. It's the story behind an inanimate object, perhaps the chair in which you now sit – not the story of the chair but of the man who made it.

There IS a feature story wherever you turn, there will be as long as there are human beings. It may be humorous, it may be tragic. The feature story ranges the human race. Its scope is unlimited, its proffered opportunity for the young journalist who wants to tell the story behind the story and tell it well also unlimited.

There is one more point to make as we leave the "approach" to feature writing:

The feature story is NOT fiction. It is based upon fact. It requires imagination but that imagination always must be geared to fact. And in this restriction, the feature writer scores against the fiction writer: To be a bit trite, truth IS stranger than fiction.

So, this is the feature story. What of the young writer beginning to learn how to write it? With what must he arm himself if he is to master the feature story?

Chapter II

The Tools

We are concerned here, you and I, with beginners in feature writing. This means you, the college student or the cub reporter in the professional field who has not been trained to write a feature story.

Whether or not you have been conscious of it, you have been reading feature stories in your newspapers and magazines and you have been listening to or seeing them on the air. Some you have enjoyed, from some you have gleaned a better understanding of the world around you, some you have laid aside because they bored you. Your reaction to them has been strictly that of the everyday reader. Now that you are learning how to write the feature story, your interest in how they are put together should be more personal. Your curiosity should be quickened.

But the work of the professional may awe the beginner. You instinctively recognize the skill in the professional's story and it may stagger you. How did he acquire that skill? The road ahead may loom long and rocky. Textbooks are filled with terminology such as narrative leads, the roller coaster technique for the body of the article, summary endings, focus and transition. And they are illustrated with examples of great stories written by the professionals.

You'll recall the suggestion that the feature writer's goal is to entertain the reader, make him comfortable. Well, suppose you and I make ourselves comfortable.

For awhile, let's continue reading the professionals for enjoyment. The time will come when you shall feel familiar enough with the construction of a feature story to dissect the professional's story to see what makes it tick. Meanwhile, let's stay in the beginners' class, realizing that the illustrations used in this book were written by beginners who had to do what you must do: Condition yourself mentally for this business of feature writing.

Now, there is nothing mysterious about this conditioning problem. It simply involves two tools every feature writer must have: Enthusiasm and curiosity.

Neither is unique to journalism; they are necessary if you are to succeed in any field of endeavor. But moreso than most, feature writing demands them. The "born" journalist has an inbred curiosity about life around him, enhanced by a natural enthusiasm for the business. "Born" journalists, however, relatively are rare. Most of us have a liking for the field but we have to manufacture the enthusiasm necessary for success. If we fail to come up with enthusiasm, we kill off the curiosity a first-class reporter must have. In feature writing, the problem might be described this way: The writer who finds an assignment dull will fail the assignment. There is no such thing as a DULL feature assignment. If you tackle each assignment with enthusiasm, whether real or manufactured, the curiosity thus generated will find the impact angle to make your copy sparkle.

A feature writer without curiosity is a carpenter without arms.

And you should be curious about the rest of the tools a beginning feature writer needs. As with enthusiasm and curiosity, the use of these tools hinges upon two words: Discipline and habit.

Here are some tools you must habitually use:

1. The dictionary — for correct spelling and word definition.
2. "Elements of Style," by Strunk & White (Macmillan) — for choice of words.
3. A thesaurus — to supplement the foregoing references.

4. Accuracy in reporting facts.
5. Correct grammar.
6. Correct punctuation.
7. Neatness.
8. Adherence to deadlines.
9. Reading.

Each of these basic tools may seem too basic to you. What is he suggesting, you may ask: That we go back to the fifth grade as a starter?

As an editor and University instructor, I find that young professional reporters and/or students and I constantly share amazement. I am amazed and appalled at their spelling, improper grammar, improper punctuation and improper use of words. They are amazed by the suggestion that they can't spell, that they use incorrect grammar and punctuation and improper words.

I should not be surprised to learn that you—the beginning feature writer-at this moment are sharing that amazement.

Nevertheless, I emphasize that you arm yourself with a dictionary. I suggest, further, that you not only obtain a comprehensive dictionary for home or office use, but a pocket dictionary as well—obviously for your pocket. As an editor, I have penalized young reporters for incorrect spelling, grammar, punctuation, and improper word usage; as a teacher, I have known university graduates to fail in job interviews because of those defects.

A would-be writer who is sloppy in this respect provokes editorial suspicion as to his accuracy. Professional and academic concern at the college and professional levels for these defects in young writers is acute.

My concern here, of course, is the development of young feature writers and not the problem, per se, of why they cannot spell or use proper grammar and punctuation and words when they reach college. To offset that problem as much as possible, I suggest the dictionary, a thesaurus and the Strunk & White textbook.

The student or young reporter might consider the fact that a lawyer never would toss off a brief without reference to his legal library; statutes and court citations are the working tools of a lawyer. Words are the working tools of a feature writer. If the established professionals use these references — and they do — certainly the beginner should.

The need for accuracy in reporting facts, as in spelling, is self-evident. A misspelled name, for example, is enough to give an editor the jitters. It aggravates the suspicion that the writer's accuracy score on other reported facts in the story is questionable.

You beginners in feature writing take note: Behind this matter of accuracy is not just the principle of professional integrity — behind it also is the threat of libel. There, too is the possibility that while distortion of a fact may not be legally libelous the ridicule it may produce is damaging not only to the target but to the reputation of publication and writer.

So, we have related these "tools" of a feature writer to such practical matters as dollars-and-cents loss to you and your publication through libel lawsuits and loss of reputation for accuracy and integrity. After all, as a feature writer in whatever field of journalism you choose you'll be writing for material gain (dollars and reputation) and publications will be printing your product for the same reason.

You will contribute to that process if your copy is neat and if you meet deadlines. I am not concerned here with your future sales success; you have to learn to write before you sell and we now are learning to write. From the outset, however, you must write "clean copy." Copy resembling the scratchings of a chicken drives editors to distraction and, worse, a dim view of you as an asset to their staffs.

Editors have infinitely less patience with the writer who fails to meet deadlines. Deadlines, too, mean dollars and cents to publishers and your failure to produce your story on time could be costly. This won't occur frequently, by the way. Once you earn the reputation of a late producer, you're on your way out.

You form the habit of using these tools through self-discipline and the cooperation of your instructor or editor. It is a dual responsibility at the outset; eventually, the responsibility solely is yours and your success will depend upon the intensity with which you strive to become a top-notch feature writer.

In no category does the element of self-discipline figure so strongly as in the matter of reading. I have suggested that for the moment you continue to read the professionals for enjoyment – until you know enough about the structure of a feature story to analyze the professional story. But the habit of reading extensively of what other writers have written and are writing must be as strong as the others. The would-be feature writer who fails to read extensively will remain a would-be feature writer.

Your instructor or editor has less control over this matter than the others. Oh, yes, the classroom instructor may assign definite, outside reading lists and, through tests, force you at least to skim through those lists. You will absorb some of what you read under pressure but you won't, as a beginner in feature writing, absorb enough of value if you meet the assignments in such manner.

What you need here, again, is enthusiasm. You must realize that the more reading of the giants of the field, past and present, you do the broader your awareness of life around you becomes. There should be, too, curiosity not only about the writers but the fields they covered or cover – and why. It could improve your understanding of this business.

What do I mean?

Assume that I have suggested two reference reading lists. One of them involves books and articles written by recognized feature writers of a half-century ago; the other includes books and articles written by recognized feature writers in the past year. Now, I'm not so naive as to think you're going to read every one of those references because I have suggested it. I'm not going to test you on them because you're going to be too busy writing to study for reading tests. Suppose I try, though, to pique your curiosity (see, that word keeps cropping up).

I suggest that you read one or two from each list, as a starter and on your own time, with two ideas in mind: (1) To read them for your own entertainment; read them through as you would any article or book you might pick up for leisurely pleasure. (2) AFTER you have read them for your entertainment, take a second look. Ask yourself: Did I LIKE the story? If so, why? What did the writer do to keep me interested from the first sentence to the last? Or, was I bored? If so, what did the writer fail to do to keep my interest? Over-all, did he get his message through to me?

As you progress in learning how to write the feature story, your answers to those questions will come more readily.

Throughout college you have been or will be exposed to the classics in literature, past and present. All this broadens your knowledge and appreciation of the art of writing.

You have studied these classics, up to now, on the basis of content and their meaning – the significance of the work. I'm suggesting now that within a relatively short time you should be examining the feature story with a critical eye not only as to content and significance but the construction of that story. HOW did the writer put it together and did he do a good job? What was the writer trying to report and did he score?

The whole idea is to educate you in the business of writing a feature story and to broaden your education. Broaden your education? I may have been a bit subtle: Therein lies another important factor. The journalist of today constantly adds to his education, during college and afterward. Today's journalism demands it. And nowhere in journalism are you given the opportunity to add to your formal education as you are in feature writing. Each assignment broadens your knowledge of life around you if you do it well.

For there is no fixed pattern to feature writing. You will cover every aspect of life. Feature writing gives you a built-in opportunity to learn as you earn and the opportunity to impart what you learn to your readers.

But, you're not there, yet!

It's time to start learning.

Chapter III

The Story Behind the Story

Late one afternoon I was alone in the COLUMBIA MISSOURIAN newsroom, working at my desk. A freckle-faced girl tripped into the room, identified herself as a high school student attending the School of Journalism's annual workshop and asked if she could use a typewriter. Of course, I said, and turned back to my work as she moved far back into the empty newsroom and sat down.

Some fifteen minutes later I became aware that there was no sound from her typewriter. She was sitting there as if in a trance, staring toward the windows.

"Young lady," I asked, "may I help you?"

She seemed startled, then asked, timidly: "Do you know anything about feature stories?"

"A little," I said.

"Well, does a feature story have to be true?"

I said, yes.

"Oh, darn," and she snapped her fingers, got up and flounced out of the room.

The youngster had been trying to dream up a fictional plot.

On another occasion I noticed in the first class session a lady from India. As I outlined the format of the course she obviously became progressively bewildered. I wasn't surprised when she followed me to my office later and asked for a consultation.

She and her husband and their baby just had arrived so that the husband could do graduate work at the University.

She was interested in writing and had decided to enroll in the feature writing course as a part-time student.

"I am puzzled," she said, "about your outline of this course. In India, we research for writing in the library. You expect your students to go out into the community, meet people and interview them. This frightens me; I know no one here and am not used to meeting people in that way. I also have my baby to consider and could not leave her for long periods."

I advised her to drop the course, to seek a writing course more in keeping with her idea of research; perhaps, after she had been in the United States awhile she might like to try our system.

On another occasion, a graduate student came to me, shaking his head:

"I have made a living writing feature stories before I came back for graduate work and I never have found it difficult to pick up feature stories on the surface. This idea of find the story BEHIND the story is foreign to me. I don't see the necessity of it."

He had been shaken by the outcome of an assignment I had given him. The assignment was a feature story about a construction crew building a road through Columbia. He had talked with the contractor and had written a routine (in what he thought was feature style) account of the progress on the project and its geographic location.

I had ordered a revision.

"I am not interested," I wrote on his copy, "in these facts which have been in the news columns. What about one of the construction workers? Why is he in the business? What is his notion of the need for the road? How did he become a construction worker? Is the pay better, say, than that of a college graduate starting out as an engineer or a clerk or in law? Or, is he a college graduate, and if so why is he wielding a pick and shovel or whatever he wields while working on that road?''

To this graduate student who had earned money writing stories about incidents he had come across accidentally, "on the surface," all this was nonsense.

These three examples illustrate misconceptions of beginners in feature writing. At least, they are misconceptions of what they are expected to learn in my course or under my editorship of a newspaper.

In feature writing, we dig for the story behind the story. Imagination is valuable, yes, but it must be imagination geared to fact. Library research is valuable, yes, but it is only part of the research formula. Of course there are readable feature stories to be found "on the surface" but women aren't going to lose their shoes down manholes every time they cross streets simply to provide a feature writer with copy.

The point is: There is a story behind every surface story. There is a story behind every human being we meet, behind every animal, behind every inanimate object whether it be a chair or wastebasket or load of cement. And these stories run the gamut of human achievement and failure, of human emotion, of war and peace. It is the job of the feature writer, in whatever form he reports to his readers, to find those stories.

The academic term for this business is research. I prefer the term, "digging for the story," or "reporting." For this is reporting in all its refinement. You, the feature writer, are going to find every fact and facet of a given assignment and — here is where the fun comes in — some facts of which neither your editor nor you was aware.

Until you have all the facts, until you have asked and have had answered the last possible question, you are not ready to write your feature story.

You may be aware by now that feature writing is not just writing. You don't write until you have the facts, including most if not all of the answers a reader logically would ask as he reads your story.

There are, of course, some fundamental rules for successful research and there are some gimmicks (tricks of the trade) to use, and it is important that you learn them. Because research or "digging" is fundamental to the feature writer's success. As you gain experience you will refine some of these rules in your own style and you will add some of your own. Feature writing is an individualistic art and while you must, as a beginner, start your career more or less on a set pattern, you quickly become a career builder unto yourself.

At this stage you ARE part of a group. As such, consider these fundamentals for research or "digging for the story."

Suppose, as a starter, we list four general sources from which you may obtain your story:

1. Records.
2. Contacts.
3. Interviews.
4. An open mind, alert to the signal to deviate from the course set by you and your editor.

Remember, as you start this research, that your ability to find the story behind the story – all the facts – and your ultimate ability to write the story constitute your "team." Your reader is not ignorant or dense. He may not be in your position to obtain all the facts but he knows when you have left a question unanswered; when that occurs, your reader is frustrated, irritated and he quickly abandons your article. Regardless of your skill as a writer, if you fail in your research to satisfy that reader, you are a failure as a feature writer.

Thoroughness is the key. And the official record is the place to start. This is true whether you are assigned to a simple newsfeature, a profile or an interpretative. For a long time human beings have been catalogued in official records, in newspaper morgues, in public libraries. Every human being has a record of some sort and we're dealing in human beings.

Suppose your assignment is a profile on John Doe. This, of course, involves an eventual interview with Mr. Doe. Your assignment is to do a word picture of John Doe, the man. And you want to know as much about him as possible BEFORE you approach him for an interview.

THIS is fundamental! For two reasons, you beginners:

(1) Knowledge of your subject makes your interview smoother, more intelligent.

(2) While your subject probably is aware that originally you hadn't known he existed, he is pleased that you have taken the trouble to check his background and this feasibly increases his willingness to cooperate.

So, John Doe has a record. Government has recorded his birth, his Social Security number, his marriage, his children if any, his voting record and any other phase of his life which has occasioned governmental attention — including a police record if any. His school and his church have records of him. If he has been recognizably successful the odds are the public library and "Who's Who" have recorded it. Newspaper morgues in his area will have their published record of his activities. And most of these records are available to you.

But the records are not enough. You are assigned to paint a complete word picture of this man. Records, cold as they are, tell much of his story but to that cold record you must add the warmth, the human element and to do that you must establish or use established contacts with the human beings who know him, know of him, through professional and social experiences: His employers, fellow employes, his friends, his enemies and, finally, his family.

This is the test of the reporter. Any reporter should be able to decipher official records (and a reporter MUST learn to do this.) Where the men are separated from the boys is this matter of contacts. Show me a first-class reporter and you show me a reporter with contacts.

The expectable limitations on a student temporarily living in a college community or a young professional reporter freshly arrived in his community do NOT excuse them from the responsibility to establish contacts as quickly as possible. As with deadline adherence, this is a habit you must acquire quickly and continue to increase your contact list as long as you are in the field.

There are as many methods of making contacts, or news sources, as there are individual reporters but two basic rules to follow might be:

(1) Figuratively put your feet on the desk of a potential news source, at his convenience and whether or not it is on your own time, and "yak" awhile and frequently.

(2) Always be honest with that potential contact, never betray his confidence. If you MUST use information he has given you confidentially, establish attribution with another source.

So it is, through your contacts – new or old – you research the blood and bones of your subject's relationship to and with his fellow citizens, with the world around him.

Now, you are ready to talk with the subject of your feature story. How do you arrange this? Call him on the telephone and say, "Look, I'm doing a feature on you and I have to talk with you. How about it?"

I am a firm admirer of the telephone; it's obviously one of the world's top inventions. But it isn't worth a whoop where the interview is concerned. I have come upon a reporter conducting a long conversation with a news source via telephone, have taken the phone from him with the order: "Get out of this office, go down to HIS office and talk with him personally!"

There is no adequate substitute for personal contact unless time or distance precludes it.

Call on your subject personally with the expectation that your first contact merely will establish a future date for the interview at HIS convenience. The value of your interview lies in time to explore every facet of your subject; to give him time to reflect, reminisce, to give studied answers to your questions based upon what you already know about him. Finally, to give him time to come up with a new angle to his word picture of which neither you nor your editor was aware even after preliminary research. You need time and that time must be at HIS convenience.

He may fool you. On your first personal contact, he may say, "No better time than now —let's talk." This shouldn't stagger you. Remember? You've learned from his records and from his friends and enemies and you're ready to talk when he is. Generally the subject appreciates your courtesy in leaving the appointment to his decision and cooperates.

I have used this functional profile assignment as an illustration of research technique. The formula holds true for whatever type of feature assignment you are given: Whether it's a newsfeature about a youngster who trained his lizard to haul his frog on a skate, the expose of a public official's professional transgression, an interview with a queen, or an interpretative on a proposed sewer bond issue.

Remember, you're after the story BEHIND the story. And always you must be alert to the possibility – sometimes I think it should be called a probability – that your digging for that story will turn up a better story than the one you originally sought. This is the intriguing aspect of feature research.

To illustrate:

I had assigned a student to do an interpretative series on the functions of municipal government offices in Columbia. Now, such a series is "old hat" in our business. I suspect there is no newspaper whose staff at one time or another hasn't written such a series. Hopefully, I crossed my fingers but actually I expected the routine report on how the city clerk issues licenses, the tax collector collects taxes, etc.

Came the day for this student to discuss her series outline with me. She seemed apprehensive. It developed that the city treasurer had claimed most of her research time demonstrating new equipment to convert the city's operation to automation. There had been no previous report on this development.

"Mr. Duffy," she said, "I have been worried sick about this. I think this automation deal is a better story for my series but I know you wanted the assignment filled as given to me."

I scarcely could refrain from shouting. Quite the contrary, I told her. I was delighted. By all means, do the automation story!

She was delighted, too, and relieved and surprised despite the fact I lectured pointedly on this possibility. Only in practical application had she learned her lesson.

Watch for that clue to a better story!

This, then, is your foundation for the feature story — digging for the story behind the story. Be alert to that last possible question and its answer, to the possible better story when and if it turns up in your research. Finally, as the research progresses, begin to form your ultimate story in your mind: The lead, the body or middle of the story, the ending — how you may organize it when you sit down to the typewriter.

This mental organization of the story during the research may be difficult for the beginner but now is the time to start training to master it. You will stumble as you learn, but you will learn to organize that story in your mind as you acquire experience and skill.

There is a formula for proving out your mental organization and this will be helpful in your early effort to train your mind in this direction. It is called the outline.

Chapter IV

The Outline

We're getting closer to the writing stage of the feature story. Getting CLOSER, I repeat. You are NOT ready to start writing. There are some important matters to resolve before you hit the typewriter.

You'll recall the reference in Chapter Two to five terms: The lead, the body or middle of the article, the ending, focus and transition. I would rearrange those terms in their order of importance to organization of the story: Focus, lead, body, ending, transition. However they are arranged, they constitute the feature story. Upon your skill in handling them hangs the success of your story. They are the keys to story organization, to the sparkle, to smooth and clear writing. To make you more comfortable, think of them as what I call the "gimmicks", the "tricks of the trade" by which a feature writer, once he masters them, rarely should fail to produce a readable story.

Remember, too, the reference in Chapter Three to mental organization of your story even as you continued the research? It was a sneaky attempt to lure you into thinking: First, what your story really is (focus); second, your lead, then what you would use in the body of the story, your ending. Finally, how you would tie it (transition) together.

If you WERE thinking, you were thinking about these things perhaps not in the specific terms but generally so. If you were NOT thinking, it is time to start now for you are at the point where you must organize your story on paper as well as in your mind.

We shall consider each of these parts of the feature story in detail later, but at this point I want you to be aware of another "gimmick" – the outline. Without it you shall find it difficult, particularly as a beginner, to recognize your story, your lead, the body of the article, and the ending. Keep in mind the suggestion that the outline is the method to prove out the soundness of the story you have been shaping mentally as you pursued the research.

I am aware, too, that you are apt to consider this outline business a chore, something of a bookkeeping job and you, impatient to get at the typewriter, could fret over the necessity of working with the outline. Well, fret if you will. But if you're smart, you'll do that outline. The professionals always use it.

Nothing irritates an editor more than a poorly organized story; nothing will bring a rejection or an order to rewrite quicker. And if there is ONE skill you as a beginner lack, it is the ability to organize a feature story.

And so, after you have ignored the advice (the odds are that you will) and have turned out a disorganized, poorly written story, try the outline!

There are, of course, as many outline systems as there are writers. The professional will use shortcuts, such as more reliance upon his mental retentive powers than upon the written detailed outline. He may use a word or two words to record a fact whereas you as a beginner may need dozens of written notes. He may use a card system: Notes on related facts grouped on one card and he may spend some time reshuffling those cards so as to follow a logical sequence as he writes the story.

He may, because he is experienced, simply sit down at the typewriter with his notes a seeming hodge-podge before him and start writing his story without a detailed outline. If he does, he probably will use this system: After writing the first draft, he will walk away from it for as long as he needs to FORGET it. When he returns, he will read that first draft objectively, as a READER – not a WRITER. The flaws in the story organization figuratively leap out of the pages at him. He rewrites, reorganizes the story in the logical sequence required.

Whatever his system, the professional knows that his story must be organized. That unless it is organized logically, the writing will not be smooth, easy on the eye, easy on the mind of the reader. When you, as the writer, jump without logic from one aspect of a story to another, the reader's eye and consequently his mind rebel. When the reader rebels, he tosses your article aside. He remembers just one thing about you and your article: Yours is ONE byline he will avoid in the future!

Getting back to you, the beginner, of course your mind is not trained, disciplined as it shall be as you acquire experience. It is for that reason I suggest the more detailed, "bookkeeping" type of outline at the outset. Such as this:

1. Jot down on a fresh sheet of paper EVERY note you have taken during your research. EVERY note, I repeat; no matter how minor it may seem.

2. On a second sheet of paper, group related notes—facts related to one another.

3. Take another look at the second list. Now you begin to separate the wheat from the chaff. Cross out in those related groups of notes facts you feel are NOT significant to your story. Do NOT destroy the discarded facts. Why? Later, as you seek your lead or ending, you could find them both among those seemingly insignificant facts! We'll come back to this point later.

4. On a third sheet of paper, jot down the significant facts you have selected, in the same related groupings.

You will note the emphasis here upon keeping related facts together. This is important for the beginner. It is vital to the smoothness of your story and while one group of related facts may seem to have little bearing upon another, by the use of transition (which also will be detailed later) you weave your story. But you will find that particularly in the body of the article there is the need to establish a major fact and finish dealing with it before you take on another.

So, you have begun to work out the organization of your story. You're now at the point where you must decide four things:

1. What IS your story?
2. What IS your lead?
3. What facts are going into the body of the article?
4. What IS your ending?

Let's begin with the question: What IS your story?

Chapter V

The Story

Simply stated, the feature writer finds his story through focus.

You know by now that research of a feature assignment uncovers any number of angles, all related in some way to the general subject and each potentially a story within itself. Your problem is to decide which single angle offers the best story to which you can anchor, through which you can illustrate the general picture of your subject. Why? Because you aim to make the reader comfortable and he is comfortable when he can "see" the story through the eyes and experiences of one person or through one aspect, say, of a scientific development.

Straight news reporters record the general picture of a national political convention, for example; feature writers bring the reader right into the scene through concentration upon one delegate or one phase of the convention activity. You make the reader feel he is THERE by such focus, you allow him the experience of putting himself in the place of a delegate whom he can understand, an everyday guy just as he, the reader, is. As you tell the story of the one delegate, the reader easily sees and understands the workings of the entire convention.

The dictionary defines focus as a "central point, as of attraction, attention, or activity." And so, you begin looking for that "central point" of your story the moment you start your research.

You are organizing your story by deciding upon what aspect you will focus and how you will weave into that story of one aspect of your assignment all the other significant angles of the story.

And you will find your big story in your outline!

Let's consider an example written by a beginner:

This student's assignment was an interpretative series on lobbyists in state capitals. Now, there are thousands of lobbyists in every seat of government in the nation; thousands of words have been written about them as a whole. The student could have fallen into the trap of generalization with an approach such as this:

There seems to be a definite place for lobbyists in our form of government. This is the consensus of legislators, the lobbyists themselves, and the public. Etcetera.

Instead, his lead on the first of three articles was:

Up on the seventh floor of the Hotel Governor in downtown Jefferson City, there's a spry old fellow — either 87 or 88, depending on the source.

"Washington says I'm 88 but the family Bible says 87. I always figured the Bible is right. After all, my mother only had eight to keep track of and Washington has millions."

Whatever his real age, A. L. McCawley is young for his years.

People who know him, and there are many, say the venerable McCawley is the granddaddy of all Missouri lobbyists. Some admiringly refer to him as the 'author of the Missouri statutes.'

From there, the student went on to tell the story of lobbyists in the Missouri state capital through the eyes of one lobbyist. This is FOCUS: Focus on ONE lobbyist in ONE state capital. By concentration on the man with a colorful background or experience in the field, the writer attracted a reader who otherwise could have been bored by a generalized lead on an oft-discussed subject.

So, we note one use of focus is to single out one of a group of persons in any given situation. Here is another way to focus:

This student was assigned to a series on what today's youth is thinking about the world around him. The writer found that the younger generation seems confused, depressed, frustrated and he could have written a generalized story about that. There have been many such studies in virtually every generation. Instead, here is how the student focused:

What does a generation sound like?

On high school and college campuses across the country, the young generation — termed apathetic, neurotic, activist, reactionary and many other things — sounds like this:

"There really isn't anything worth doing."

"My only goal is to make $12,000 a year."

"I have to live from day to day because I don't know if there'll be a tomorrow."

"I will consider myself a success if I can develop a happy philosophy of life and be a good mother."

"So far my education has been meaningless because I live only from one test to another and don't have time to ask why or to really know what I'm doing."

Note that the writer concentrated on ONE aspect of his subject: What does a generation SOUND like? He carried this theme throughout his series, using quotes from individuals with telling effect — much more telling than if he had tackled the generation as a whole.

You will recall the example in Chapter One, the writer assigned to a story on the current popularity of fine arts:

There are more painters in the United States than there are hunters.

More people play the piano than hold fishing licenses. Etcetera.

That was FOCUS!

Consider the student assigned to do a profile on an aged man. Advanced age is the signal for many feature stories in any community. These stories usually report how long the subject has or has not been smoking or drinking or chopping wood. Here was this student's approach:

He was sitting in the parlor, slightly bent with arthritis, white hair cut short and neatly trimmed. On the wall hung a marriage license. It's faded now but the words are legible: ___ and ___ . They had met that year when he came to Columbia and began work as a printer. She worked upstairs in the proof room. They were married in the same room where the license now hangs. They lived together in this house almost 50 years; in the bedroom, on ___ , she died in his arms.

"I always said I was going to marry a sure enough woman and that's what I did and that's why it hurts so much. Oh, she was a nice girl!"

That was FOCUS! Focus on one aspect of an aged man's life and the result was a story which grasped the reader at once and held him.

Focus is the tool by which the feature writer takes his story out of the mine-run pattern of everyday writing. It is the dramatization of an aspect of everyday life. It provides the spice, the color. It produces the story behind the story.

And you'll note that these examples have something in

common in addition to the story behind the story. Each puts the reader at ease by zeroing in on a situation in which the reader can place himself comfortably – whether it makes him laugh or weep in sympathy. The situation is understandable, the language is understandable. You will find as we progress that you will be using focus in that meaning – clarity of understanding – throughout your story. You will be using focus to reduce technical jargon and situations to everyday language and situations by comparison, making it easier for the reader to "see" the word picture you are painting.

The fact that all of these examples obviously provided colorful leads for the writers should prepare you to recognize as we go along that these five parts of the feature story form a close-knit family; one leads into another and continues to thread its way throughout the story, picking up the others as it proceeds.

Let's begin the threading process. You have decided through focus upon the central theme of your story. It is time to look for the lead.

Chapter VI

Leads and Endings

I am not being unconsciously trite when I say that history repeats itself. On the surface, that is. And feature writers realize this early in their careers as they fret over new twists to old stories, situations in their communities which have been covered time and again not only there but elsewhere in the world. New generations do much as the preceding generations did: They are born, they go to school, they marry, they die. In the course of those basic functions they variously laugh, cry, maim and kill each other depending upon the course world history should be taking during their lifetimes.

Yet, each generation does those things a bit differently and it is the test of the feature writer to find the difference. You will recall in Chapter Five the examples of focus. In each instance, the writer dealt with basically commonplace situations. His story sparkled only because he found a new twist, an improvement however slight on the way similar stories had been told earlier.

For instance, some years ago I assigned a new reporter to interview the last survivor of the Civil War in our community. The youngster talked with the veteran, returned to the office and knocked out an obviously routine yarn about the man's experiences in the Union Army, how he had returned to civilian life in 1865 and had married, sired fourteen children — all the usual stuff. And he started his story this way:

John Doe, 102 years old yesterday, sees the world today as not much better than he saw it in 1865.

Well, Civil War veterans had been seeing the world that way since the first interview with one of them. They also had been reporting their return to civilian life, their family experiences for as long. I called the reporter to the desk and told him so. He listened politely, gave me the stock answer: "What else is there to tell?" And then, as he started to walk away he said, "Brother! What an optimist that old geezer is!"

"Why?"

"Y'know what he did yesterday? He ordered a brand new uniform!"

The reporter did a double take, stared at me as the light dawned. And he rewrote his lead!

He had been so bored with his assignment he hadn't made a note of the fact at the time the old man mentioned it. Neither had this youngster made even a hurried outline of what he had learned. Had it not been for the fact registering on his subconscious, he would have lost the only fresh fact he had found.

And need a fresh fact, he did! As you will need the fresh fact, the new twist, the PUNCH in your lead AND your ending!

I have emphasized how close-knit the five vital parts of a feature story are and you will be more acutely aware from this point how true that is. Each IS vital to the feature story. The writer walks the tightrope from the moment he types the first sentence to the moment he types the last sentence. At any point between, he can lose the reader. When your instructor or editor tells you that you can fail in the lead, in the body of the article, in the ending he is giving you sound advice.

Because it comes first, after you have decided upon your story theme, the lead accordingly becomes here your first concern. And because they are so alike in treatment, we shall consider the ending in the same package.

The intriguing thing about your lead, you will learn, is its uncertainty; in a sense it is unpredictable. This will be true most often, until you have your outline perfected and you start hunting for that fact with the PUNCH element in it. Oh, there will be times when the lead stands out almost from the beginning of your research. This will not occur frequently.

You know the central theme of your story and now you study the outline for a clue to the fact with the new twist, the PUNCH. You will see that word PUNCH here repeatedly because it is is vital. Without it in the lead, there is little hope you will attract the reader, certainly that you will keep his interest.

Remember the warning NOT to discard those facts you had decided were not vital to the story? This is another intriguing aspect of the lead. In those facts you have set aside you well may have your lead!

The same is true of your ending.

So, study your outline – with special attention to those insignificant facts you had culled from your original notes. You are looking for the twist, the PUNCH!

There are two other points to keep in mind as you search for the lead:

(1) Your lead and your ending must relate to the whole story.

(2) Unlike a straight news story, your feature lead may require a sentence or several paragraphs. Where a straight news story is paragraphed frequently, for easier reading of its staccato style, the relaxed and smoother approach to a subject in a feature story makes a paragraph a unit of thought, a lead a unit of thought and until you are ready to dip into the body of your article, however many paragraphs you have written still constitutes the lead.

Here's an example:

This student did a profile. His lead was:

I. C. Adams Jr. probably never will set the world
on fire. Not because he doesn't have the intelligence
(he was offered a job to teach ornithology at a university and has 180 hours of college credits). Nor
because he doesn't have the business sense (he started a mail order used book business and was instru-
mental in starting two other men in the used book
business). Nor because he doesn't have the winning
personality (his shop, Adams Books & Hobbies,
214 North Eighth St., is Columbia's general store
minus the pot bellied stove). Gun, book, stamp, coin
and junk collectors stop in all day to chat, barter or
haggle with I.C.

No, I.C. (that's his legal name) won't set the world
afire because he's too fond of living, bird watching,
hunting, flying, trading and collecting to step aboard
the treadmill of success.

From this point, the writer launched into the body of his
story. Incidentally, his transition from the lead to the body
was faulty, and we'll consider that problem later. His lead,
though, was valid and well done. His twist, the word picture
of a man who was not trying to make a fortune, was calculated to intrigue the reader. It set the theme of the profile
and that is what a good lead should do.

This student worried a great deal about his lead. His
subject seemed to the inexperienced writer to offer him
little fodder for a punch lead. Eventually, the student
realized that the story lay within the subject's disregard
for material gain in favor of doing what he liked to do. You
must be alert to this trait of human nature. There is a
story and a punch lead in the man who prefers to sit under
a tree and watch the world go by.

And so, the young writer came up with what might be called a summary lead, one of a number of rather set patterns for leads (until you are skilled enough to vary the pattern to the point where critics rave over your leads without being able to classify them). Some of the others are the narrative lead, the descriptive lead, the direct approach lead, the quotation lead.

As we consider these types of leads, be aware of the twists to them, the punch for regardless of what label you put on your lead, if it doesn't have that punch it's dead!

Here is another example of the summary lead:

There's nothing on the surface to distinguish "Pill Hill" from any other residential area in the southern part of Columbia. Bordered on the east by a meandering Flat Branch Creek and the straight-laced Missouri Kansas-Texas Railroad tracks, on the south by the Outer Loop, on the west by Greenwood Avenue, and on the north by Rollins Avenue it was dubbed "Pill Hill" because so many University doctors and professors live there.

The "surface" is misleading.

By emphasis upon the unique tag of "Pill Hill" and why it is called that and the use of the one sentence – The "surface" is misleading – the writer has attracted an audience. The reader will continue reading because he wants to know WHY the surface is misleading.

Consider this student's problem with a summary lead. Her assignment was a story on a scheduled state-wide high school student council convention. Her first effort:

Brother, can you spare a bed, or two or three – a floor, Aunt Hildy's old quilt? Even a smidgen of sleeping space would be enough for the boys and girls who will be coming to Columbia for a convention of the Missouri Association of student councils.

It might as well have been a classified ad. And I wrote on her paper: "Now for a REAL feature story, why not focus on one person's experiences in planning this event?"

Her second effort:

Plodding through the slush to get an estimate on potato chips is just part of a day's work for Vicky Riback.

Vicky, a senior at University High School and co-chairman of the March 13 Student Council convention, is a girl on the go. With the responsibility of meeting, greeting and housing 850 teen-aged visitors, Vicky hasn't much time to relax.

From there, the writer took Vicky through typical experiences in this project, including her reference in the body of the story to the housing problem: "We'll be dead if we don't get some beds!"

Another example of a lead calculated to draw the reader into a familiar situation and thus intrigue him is this one:

Bob Smith, a senior in high school, dashed into the public library at 7 o'clock one night to do some research on the "magic clock" for a class report the next day. After an hour of feverish and futile search, he asked the librarian for help. She checked available records and said the library had no information on the subject.

Although this is a theoretical situation, it reflects the serious problem facing many of Missouri's 144 public libraries – that of limited library resources and references.

This might be called a narrative lead. It simply sets a "scene" in your lead, by which you draw the reader into personal contact as witness to a situation establishing the theme of your story. Here is another example:

One day in late August, Alfred Novak was standing in a washroom in Amherst, Mass., getting ready to shave.

He spotted a friend, Herman Muller, already busy shaving five sinks away.

"Herman," the graying Novak asked, "how would you like to take part in an experiment?"

The Nobel Prize-winning biologist turned to listen.

"You would give a lecture over the telephone to people more than a thousand miles away."

Muller agreed and four months of lining up lecturers ended there in the washroom.

And another:

A 16-year-old student entered a phone booth in Birmingham. He paused a moment, then nervously instructed the operator to connect him with his parents in Ashland, Ill.

"Hello, Mom. Guess what? I dropped out of school and I'm in Alabama. I think I'm going to get a job on a ship and travel around the world with a couple of guys."

Silence....then, "you WHAT?"

"They really weren't too upset," Charles Beadles said as he sat in his office at the State Farm Insurance Co. and recalled an adventure of his youth. "I left Illinois Wesleyan University after my third semester. My parents agreed that I shouldn't come back to settle down until I had the wanderlust out of my system."

And another:

It's Monday morning in Jefferson City. In the Capitol the elevators are crowded — almost a small version of state government within themselves. A governor's assistant nods good morning to a representative of a pressure group. A legal expert lifts his hat to a secretary. Two out-of-town guests here for a conference speak softly to each other.

The elevator stops and people quickly disappear down the corridors and into doors lettered in gilt.

One man who gets off carries no briefcase or crammed file folder. He, too, turns into a gold-lettered door. Yet, this man is not paid by the state. He is not a lobbyist. Nor is he a guest. But his presence in the Capitol is vital to the democratic process.

The letters on the door he enters spell PRESS. He is a state capitol correspondent.

The descriptive lead is in a class to itself. Generally, I advise beginners in feature writing to avoid it until they have acquired enough practical experience and have developed their own style. It is the type of lead you find in fiction and feature writers habitually make the same mistake as unseasoned fiction writers: They overdo it and the result is reader boredom.

The key to the descriptive lead is simplicity so as to give the reader a clear, uncluttered picture of a particular scene and then only when such a setting seems pertinent to the lead theme of your story. I was amazed by a descriptive lead on a student's story only once. Her assignment was a series on the Missouri farmer and her lead was a beautiful description of a dust storm hitting a corn field. And then came her acknowledgement (in the story) that it was an excerpt from John Steinbeck's "Grapes of Wrath."

Beginners can use the descriptive lead in its simplified form, however. Here are a couple of examples I approved:

Imagine a summer day with the temperature in the high 90's. The lawns are turning yellow, the car needs to be washed, there are piles of dirty dishes and laundry, Aunt Sarah wants to take her Saturday night bath and, most of all, you'd like a cool drink of water.

But there is no water.

A cell – the world of the law breaker. A man caged in a barren, rectangular enclosure, with three gloomy green walls and a stretch of equally spaced bars from ceiling to floor across the front.

This is what struck me the first time I entered a jail. It wasn't filthy, nor was it dark or damp. There was no shouting, singing or humming. I only could hear whispering tones. But I felt the penetrating stare of eyes that followed me down the corridors as I was escorted to a cell.

I was scared, uneasy, as I was paraded past the cells. I was an outsider, just looking in. I didn't know what to expect.

The direct approach lead is the most comfortable of all for beginners, yet you must beware of overdoing it. This is the "gimmick" whereby you address the reader directly, draw him into the discussion at once. An example:

Does your medicine cabinet resemble an overstocked pill manufacturer's supply warehouse?

Do your bureau drawers remind you of a showroom overflowing with the latest in candy-coated, fruit-flavored vitamin capsules?

Ladies, do your pocketbooks bulge from all the bottles and pill boxes containing this power-packed vitamin for now and that vitamin compound for an after-lunch snack?

Is your stomach so full of vitamin tablets you don't
have an appetite?

Are you annoyed because your children use their red,
blue and pink vitamin pills for money in their game of
Monopoly?

Do you spend so much time chomping on vitamins
every day that you forget to take your ulcer pill?

If you nod your head in agreement, you are a vitamin
victim.

Consider this lead:

Have you heard the old joke about the drunk who
staggered out of a party and tried to drive home?

"You're not going to drive home in that condition?"
a concerned friend asked.

"Of course (hic) I am," the drunk replied. "I'm in
no condition (hic) to walk."

The moment this drunk staggers into his car, starts
his engine and peels onto the highway – the joke ends.
Wrapped in his shaky hands is 3,500 pounds of steel
which can kill a human being as efficiently as a high-
powered rifle in the hands of an assassin.

Finally, there is the quotation lead. Here, again, you
must be careful in how you handle it. If the quotation you
use lacks the twist, the punch, you lose the reader.

An example of a quotation lead with a punch:

"I stay at the library until it closes," the girl
shivered. "Then I come home and go to bed fully
dressed."

The girl, a psychology major at the university, looked

around her room. It wasn't much. A tiny desk in the
corner, a cream-colored bureau with its top crusted
with stains from glasses and mugs, a kitchen chair.

She was sitting on the bed and she was wrapped in her
winter coat.

"It warms up a little bit in the daytime," she said.
"But, brother, trying to get up in the morning when
it's below zero outside takes all the will power I
have."

She laughed: "Oh well, I expect it's good for the soul.
And there's not much I can do about it right now."

She pays $35 for this room which is four blocks from
campus. It is one of several student rooms on the top
floor of a house built in the 19th Century. The house
is old and in deplorable condition. It never was de-
signed to have students crammed into every corner.

Here's another way to use the quotation lead:

There used to be a lawyer who argued his cases by
quoting authority from the Bible. But one time he
didn't. The presiding judge asked why.

"Why," said the lawyer, "this court has overruled
the Bible so many times, I don't consider the Bible
an authority any more."

Well, it's true that the Missouri Supreme Court
doesn't draw its authority from the Bible. Instead,
it relies upon hundreds of court opinions which Justice
S.P. Dalton says, "We are buried herewith."

One more example:

"If you want to get sick, go to a doctor!"

These words were not spoken in malice or anger by
a bed-ridden invalid. It simply is the philosophy of
healthy, 96-year-old John Morgan Wright who never
has been really sick and refuses to take medicine.

All of these leads, regardless of the category, reflect

a common quality – PUNCH! All of them set the stage for the rest of the story. Your endings also must have PUNCH. They must maintain the pace you set throughout the article.

Generally there are two types of endings: The summary and what most writers call the snapper or unusual twist ending. Whichever type you use, there is one trap to avoid– editorialization. It is a trap into which beginners fall repeatedly. It is a lazy way to end a story and you couldn't leave a reader with a worse taste in his literary mouth. You, particularly, as a beginner are NOT qualified to pass judgment upon a person or a situation. Years hence, if you have become a recognized authority in one field or another, the reader may be interested in your personal opinion. At this stage of your career, he couldn't be less interested.

There is a vast difference in what you as a reporter relay what you have seen and what you as an individual think of what you have seen.

In the student examples of endings I shall record in a moment, you will note the lack of personal opinion as to whether a subject is a "great man" or a situation is "extremely acute and someone must do something about it," etc. In all cases attribution to an authority – particularly the subject himself – is used. Let's consider some of these examples.

Remember the lead on the profile of the man who "probably never will set the world on fire"? We pick up the story as the writer approaches the ending:

> "This book dealer stayed all day and found eight books that he offered to buy for a nickel apiece. I wanted $50 for them. He left and called later and offered me $40 for them but I told him the price had gone to $60. The books don't eat anything so I wasn't in a rush to sell them."

> Today, I.C. leads the life of an independent man. He buys what he wants, sells what he can make a profit

on, travels during August through the West trading
at gun shows and watching birds. He doesn't cloud
his day with great plans but just drifts along, thinking maybe one day he will resume prospecting or bird
watching in Africa or Alaska.

This is a summary ending which maintains the theme of
the story, as the lead had set the stage for it. It leaves the
reader with a pleasant memory of a relaxed, easy-going
man whom the reader quite probably would like to know.

Then, there was the girl university student freezing in
her attic room. The ending was:

The girl is caught in the squeeze between enormous
growth in university enrollment and the frantic pace
of housing to keep up. She keeps her ear to the ground
waiting to find a better place. By next year she hopes
to have found a better room or apartment she can
share.

But in the small, cold room on the third floor, another
freezing student will take her place.

The student assigned to the Missouri Supreme Court
story approached his ending this way:

If the vote is to concur, the Supreme Court upholds
the lower court's decision. In this case, if the ap-
pellant still feels he is right he can take it to the
U.S. Supreme Court. If the state Supreme Court re-
verses and remands the lower court decision, the case
must be retried. "Judges who have their opinions
reversed," Justice Leedy says, "take it as a matter
of course. Of course, there was one irritated judge
who said,'Well, you just had the last guess!' "

Guesswork is not the forte of the Supreme Court.

And the ending to the story of the 96-year-old man who
refuses to take medicine:

Wright has lived a contented life. Perhaps his happiest moment was when he and his wife celebrated 50 years of marriage in 1953. They were allowed eight more years together before Mrs. Wright died in December, 1961.

Her death took away part of Wright's heart but not his love. His voice trembled slightly as he talked of her and the tears escaped his dimming eyes and fell shamelessly onto his chest — symbols of the love he still cherishes.

Life has been, obviously, a beautiful experience for John Morgan Wright — not a burden.

The theme of the story about the drunken driver concerned a legislature's debate over stricter laws. The writer's ending:

In the Senate where lawyers dominate, questions of constitutionality often are argued, but usually debate is calm.

In 1963, debate turned into a fight.

The questions were many, the replies swift. But throughout the debate, one question plagued the senators: How many will die because of drunk driving next year?

There was no reply to this swift question.

These examples have been summary endings. They "sum up" what has been written throughout the story, from the lead through the body of the article to the ending. In much the same way, the snapper ending—the ending with a twist as well as punch — serves the same purpose. It is related to the entire story.

In the story about the veteran lobbyist in the Missouri

state capital, the student wrote this ending:

> Even after more than 60 active years in Jefferson
> City it is difficult for an old lobbyist to call it quits.
> He retired from his position with the Society of
> Engineers two years ago and isn't building bridges
> any more. But he isn't through.
>
> "Now," he says with a twinkle in his eye, "I'm
> building nursing homes."

Another student did a story about the U.S. Weather
Bureau, how the meteorologists send radio-equipped bal-
loons skyward to collect data on atmospheric conditions.
Along the way, the help this affords pilots is described. The
possible effect of the weather on the crime rate and upon
animals is discussed. And the ending went this way:

> Can the average Joe predict his own weather?
>
> The Weather Bureau discounts weather lore, but
> Clark Ellzey, a private airplane pilot, thinks man can
> do a little predicting on his own.
>
> "I go out in the morning and throw my hat in the air.
> If it doesn't come back, I know not to fly that day!"

The story about the young generation and "what does it
sound like" – remember? Here's the ending:

> Obviously a generation as complex as this one can-
> not be typed or classified or simply dismissed with a
> generalization. Those who have called today's youth
> the "so what? generation", the "nervous generation"
> or the "tormented generation", may be more intent
> on naming it than understanding it.
>
> As one student commented, "why do they always have
> to name every generation? The youth of the Twenties
> were called the 'lost generation' and produced some

of the greatest American art and literature yet. They
weren't lost and neither are we. I think we're the
most NAMED generation!''

Leads and ending with PUNCH!

So, you have found your lead and your ending; your outline indicates what you want to put into the body of your
article. And when you come to this point, the point of putting
your whole article in proper organization, you must worry
about two things: How to write the body of the article and
how to cement the lead, body, and ending in smooth, coherent writing. And transition, the fifth member of the feature
article family, provides the cement.

Chapter VII

The Whole Story

Now that you have selected your lead and your ending, you must "fill the gap" — organize and write the body of your article. This means you are ready to write the whole story.

It means, too, that you must tie that story together, smoothly, coherently, figuratively leading the reader by the hand from one segment of your story to the other in a way he, the reader, can follow you comfortably. It means now you are going to use transition.

You see, you don't write a feature story in three parts. It isn't a business such as making a movie, in which you shoot a scene designated for the middle of the picture one day, the opening scene the next, the closing scene the next and then all the other middle scenes the final day. There is no film cutter to put all your tidbits together in sequence after the shooting is done. YOU are the organizer and when you have your lead in mind, what you want in the body or middle of the article and the ending well in mind and supported by a logical outline, you sit down to the typewriter and write the WHOLE story.

Quickly, you will learn that one of your problems with a lead, no matter how sparkling it may be, is to find a means to leave it and smoothly and logically enter the body of the story. Throughout the body of the story, as you cover major points, you will need this smooth transition from one point to another; when you are ready for the ending, you must use transition to connect the body with the ending as you have connected the lead with the body.

Taking first steps first, let us consider the problem of connecting the lead with the body of the article.

51

I mentioned in Chapter Six a transitional problem in the story about "Pill Hill." Here was the difficulty:

The student writer's first effort:

There's nothing to distinguish "Pill Hill" with any other residential area in the southern part of Columbia. Bordered on the east by a meandering Flat Branch Creek and the straight-laced Missouri-Kansas-Texas Railroad tracks, on the south by the Outer Loop, on the west by Greenwood Avenue, and on the north by Rollins Avenue, it was dubbed "Pill Hill" because so many University doctors and professors live there.

Of the 74 families who live on Red Bud Lane, Greenwood Avenue, Glenwood Court, and Lakeshore Drive, 60 of them belong to a private group: The Quarry Heights Owners Association.

Do you recognize the lack of coherence in those two paragraphs? What, the reader will ask as his mind is jerked from the observation that "Pill Hill" resembles any other area to the report that 60 of the 74 families belong to an association, has one to do with the other? The addition of seven words transformed the lead and opening paragraph of the body of the article into coherent, logical sequence. Those seven words are the transitional means of achieving logic and unity in thought. Here is the revised version:

There's nothing ON THE SURFACE to distinguish "Pill Hill" from any other residential area in the southern part of Columbia. Bordered on the east by a meandering Flat Branch Creek and the straight-laced Missouri-Kansas-Texas Railroad tracks, on the south by the Outer Loop, on the west by Greenwood Avenue, and on the north by Rollins Avenue, it was dubbed "Pill Hill" because so many University doctors and professors live there.

THE "SURFACE" IS MISLEADING.

Of the 74 families who live, etc.

See the difference? The capitalized words set the stage for the story in the lead and smoothly enable the reader to follow the theme — that this is an unusual neighborhood — from the lead into the body of the story. This is transition!

Remember the profile on the man who doesn't want to set the world afire? The second and final paragraph of the student's lead was:

No, I.C. (that's his legal name) won't set the world afire because he's too fond of living, bird watching, hunting, flying, trading and collecting to step aboard the treadmill of success.

From that point, in the next paragraph the writer jumped abruptly into this:

I.C., or Ike as some call him, was born in Columbia in 1913 to Mr. and Mrs. Ira C. Adams who operated an antique shop. But I.C. says, "I didn't take much interest in it."

Can you imagine the reader mentally trying to follow a disconnected thought such as, "born in Columbia in 1913, he wasn't interested in his parents' antique shop." The addition of eight words between the second and third paragraphs made sense out of incoherence:

No, I.C. (that's his legal name) won't set the world afire because he's too fond of living, bird watching, hunting, flying, trading and collecting to step aboard the treadmill of success.

HE'S ALWAYS BEEN THAT WAY. FOR INSTANCE:

I.C., or Ike as some call him, was born in Columbia in 1913 to Mr. and Mrs. Ira C. Adams who operated an antique shop. But I.C. says, "I didn't take much interest in it.'' It wasn't what he wanted to do, simply said. Instead, the blue-eyed boy started collecting stamps, studying and watching birds and getting acquainted with nature.

There are a number of pat phrases and words the feature writer may use to effect transition. Some of them are:

Why?
For instance.
In that respect.
By the way.
For example.
If you think that was typical, consider this. . . . .
If he had any better ideas about it, he abandoned them
 for. . . . .

Generally, the more original the writer can make his transitional words, phrases or sentences the more appreciative is the reader who is able to travel from segment to segment of the story in mental comfort.

Now, before we put the article together, by use of examples, let's consider the body of the article.

Have you ever covered a speech? The experienced reporter knows that all orators change the pace, break up their speeches, say, between the serious and the light veins. The orator use jokes, for example, as his tool. He also changes the pace by establishing a major point and then elaborating on that point.

To maintain reader interest in the body of the article, and this is mandatory if you are to keep that reader with you, the feature writer uses this technique. What some writers call the roller coaster or mountains-and-valleys method of writing the body of the article simply is this formula: Establish a major point (the mountain) and explain it (the valley). Then, by the use of transition establish another major point, explain it, and so on.

It particularly is in this phase of your story that you utilize focus to reduce story situations to understandable language and comparable situations more readily "seen" by the reader.

There is nothing awesome about this as you will see in the following examples of stories written by beginners, just as you are, after they had understood the mechanics of the feature story and had learned through close consultation with their instructors and editors to put it all together.

In these examples, I shall capitalize the transitional words, phrases or sentences and designate by marginal notes the major points.

Example No. 1:

Bob Smith, a senior in high school, dashed into the public library at 7 o'clock one night to do some research on the "magic clock" for a scientific report due in class the next day. After an hour of feverish and futile search, he asked the librarian for help. She checked available sources and said the library had no information on the subject.

Focus on one Aspect

ALTHOUGH THIS IS a theoretical situation, it reflects the serious problem facing many of Missouri's 144 public libraries – that of limited library resources and references.

MISSOURI doesn't stand alone in this battle for quality library service, and the state doesn't stand still. To tackle this pressing problem effectively, a survey (sponsored by the Missouri Library Association (MLA)) to determine where reform and improvement were needed was conducted in 1962. An analysis of the survey by the MLA development committee disclosed three sources of pressure which constantly create or lead to inadequate state public library services:

Elaboration

1. Increased demands for more difficult reference services and specialized information needs of new industries.

2. Students increasing their use of public libraries as a result of stepped-up school programs.

3. A shift of population centers to large urban areas.

IN OTHER WORDS, more persons are utilizing more library services and requesting more reference services than currently are available; in addition to a population shift which is causing a more severe problem of limited library resources.

Major Point

A state-wide library plan has been developed, BASED ON THE FINDINGS OF THE SURVEY. It would establish a system of inter-related libraries with inter-related functions and services. At the apex of this system would be the services and resources afforded by the Missouri State Library in Jefferson City.

Elaboration

The essence of THIS LIBRARY PLAN is three major resource libraries linked to 15 system libraries located in the state's major trade areas which, in turn, would be related to numerous area and community libraries. Every public library in the state, although a separate system, would be in a state-wide library system, related to all other library resources in the state.

THUS, the large libraries with valuable resources would share their services and resources with other libraries on an equitable basis. The objective: Quality library service for all Missourians.

Focus by Comparison

COMPARE THIS LIBRARY SYSTEM with a winding road up a steep mountain. At the foot of the mountain are the many community libraries with their exceptionally limited resources. One mile up the mountain are the area libraries. At this point, the view is broadened and a traveler may see a winding river he was unable to see at the foot of the mountain. His perspective has been expanded somewhat.

TWO MILES HIGHER, the system libraries are located. From this height, it is possible to see a large metropolis on the far side of the river gleaming in the sun. Again, a traveler benefits from the additional level attained. As the traveler reaches the top of the mountain where the major resource libraries are, his vision sweeps the ocean stretching into the horizon.

THE TOP OF THE MOUNTAIN offers unlimited knowledge and resources for the traveler who could not be completely satisfied with the limited resources lower down the mountain.

The Missouri State Library and the St. Louis and Kansas City Public Libraries would be the "TOP OF THE MOUNTAIN." They would serve as the three major resource libraries with unlimited resources, outstanding reference services and reserve pools of information for the people throughout the state. Ideally, any book or service requested by one of the smaller libraries should be available at one of these resource centers.

Currently the State Library does not have the exceptional resources TO BE FOUND IN THE OTHER TWO LARGE LIBRARIES, and legislative appropriations will be necessary before the State Library can become effective as a major resource center. The St. Louis and Kansas City Public Libraries are endowed with a mammoth population that provides sufficient revenue for quantity resources.

IF THIS LIBRARY PLAN should go into effect (reports indicate within two years), the State Library would have special responsibilities for promotion and maintenance. According to MLA's "Guide to Library Development", the State Library would promote the development of a genuine, state-wide program of library service and conduct research in a "strong, service-minded and leadership-oriented" manner.

The State Library also would be charged to maintain a "collection which supplements and reinforces the resources of library systems." This would include: Central reports, government and civilian documents, audio-visual material and information and reference services to government departments, agencies, and projects. The State Library also would serve as a storage center for little used material from all libraries.

Major
Point

Exceptionally important IN THIS NETWORK would be the 15 system libraries. These libraries correspond with the cultural, trade and socio-economic centers of the state based on 1962 statistics. They would incorporate 13 existent regional libraries and function as the administrative center for a large area encompassing several counties.

Elaboration

ON THE OTHER HAND, area libraries would serve communities encompassing a secondary trade area or densely populated urban section. These libraries would request books and services from the nearest system library and would share their own resources with community libraries.

COMMUNITY LIBRARIES are at the bottom of the "mountain." They serve hundreds of persons populating small communities. Their resources would be limited to a narrow range of materials and services. Thus, community libraries would rely upon area libraries to supplement their own resources.

A final noteworthy aspect of THIS PROPOSED LIBRARY PLAN is an extension of existent extra services. This would mean higher quality bookmobile and special book collection services. These specialized services must be improved consistently along with the library system so that quality services will be available to all Missourians.

Ending

IN ALL THIS PLANNING, Missouri's library leaders are upholding traditions established by their predecessors: Establishment of progressive public library programs. Although library development was retarded in contrast to other states, Missouri benefited from the experiences of older states. As one result, the theory of cooperative library services became a reality in Missouri.

Today, the leaders again are cooperating to provide

inter-related, quality library service to all Missourians. A major part of their success will depend upon the financial support of the Legislature.

################

While this example is not one calculated to make the reader laugh uproariously or weep copiously, the subject is one affecting the population at large. Of more importance, it embodies all of the mechanics needed to produce a smooth feature story, as the notations stress.

Example No. 2 is an excerpt from an interpretative series on the drunken driver and the debate in the legislature over proposals to stiffen the traffic laws. Again, transition is capitalized. Again, focus is used to make it easier for the reader to "see" the situation.

Example No. 2:

Have you heard the old joke about the drunk who staggered out of a party and tried to drive home?

"You're not going to drive home in that condition?" a concerned friend asked.

"Of course I am," the drunk replied. "I'm in no condition (hic) to walk."

The moment THIS DRUNK staggers into his car, starts the engine and peels onto the highway – the joke ends. Wrapped in his shaky hands is 3,500 pounds of steel which can kill a human being as efficiently as a high-powered rifle in the hands of an assassin. — Focus by Comparison

Sitting behind the wheel, he is PLACING HIS FINGER ON THE TRIGGER. With his reflexes slow, vision dim and self confidence climbing, he builds his courage. Weaving down the highway at 100 m.p.h., he is taking aim. Whether or not he means to – he kills.

Major
Point

THE FACTS speak for themselves:

A 19-year-old girl was killed when the car in which she was a passenger was struck from the rear by another car.

Two women were killed when their car was struck head-on by another car.

A 7-year-old girl was killed when a car jumped the curb.

These drivers were drunk.

Elabora-
tion

Missouri law enforcement officers call it D.W.I. – driving while intoxicated. The mother of the dead 7-year-old girl calls it just plain drunk.

Major
Point

WHATEVER ITS NAME, the results are usually the same.

"Out of 22,019 accidents our department worked in 1962 and a similar amount in 1963, about 22 per cent of the people involved were drinking," Col. Hugh Waggoner, superintendent of the Missouri Highway Patrol, says. "Of the 1,017 fatal accidents, our figures indicate that around 40 per cent of the people involved had been drinking."

Elabora-
tion

THESE STATISTICS emphasize an old but true saying about highway accidents: Twenty per cent of the drivers cause 80 per cent of the accidents.

This applies to the drunken driver. He can kill himself and take two, three, four, even five other lives. This is the real tragedy, the innocent who pay for the crimes of the guilty with the highest medium of exchange – their lives.

"We are not as bad as people say, and we have better traffic laws than many other states," Col. Waggoner says. "But we have one costly weakness – poor drunken driving laws."

Major
Point

In the last few years, THIS WEAKNESS has been so costly that people are beginning to ask: How can we get drunken drivers off the road?

"Convict them!" cries an angry citizen.

"Punish them!" pleads a mourning mother.

"How?" prosecuting attorneys ask. "How do we get drunks off the road if we can't get convictions? How do we get convictions without evidence? How do we get evidence?"

Answer these questions and the problem is solved. Right now the answers are vague.

################

From there the writer dipped deeper into the body of his story. He cited the law and the opinions of law enforcement officers and courts to pinpoint the vagueness of those answers. From these, he wove his story into the legislative debate.

Notice, again, how each of these writers would establish a major point in the body of the story, explain it, weave it into the next major point. Notice, too, how the writer in Example No. 2 enlivened his body text with quotations — colorful quotations which had significance to the story theme. And each of them used focus to make the reader "see" more readily the word picture the writer was painting by comparing a story situation with a situation more familiar to the everyday citizen.

Focus and transition!

They are the twins which provide the color and the cement to make your story from start to finish the smoothly written article with the spark to attract the reader in the first sentence and retain his interest through the last sentence.

In the final analysis, though, the focus, the lead, the body of the story, the ending and transition are composed of words. And words are the tools of the feature writer. How he uses them spells the quality of his story.

Let's look at words.

Chapter VIII

Choice of Words

Throughout this discussion of the feature story I have emphasized the need to make the reader comfortable, relaxed. I think it is as important that the writer be comfortable. His rapport with the reader should be easier if he is.

This includes the writer and his feeling for the words he uses.

You, the beginner, may find this business of word usage and grammer a bit confusing at first. Relax: You are not alone. You will realize, eventually, that rarely do two grammarians agree on every point. That the changing world has changed for the man on the street the exact definition of all too many words in the English vocabulary. There will be other obstacles. You will find that instructors and editors frequently disagree on such matters; that they also disagree on what constitutes a feature story and particularly on the style in which you write it. There are editors who are feature-prone and there are editors who refuse to recognize anything not written in the straight news format. There, too, is the matter of writing in the style each publication prefers.

Yes, this may confuse you at first. I subscribe to the observation frequently made by a colleague: "It is good for your soul." And so it is. The sooner you become aware of these differences, these problems ahead of you, the better.

You must discipline yourself to awareness of the problems and adjustment to them as you meet them under individual editors and publications. It is not difficult if you gear yourself to flexibility. After all, even the grammarian has come around to a certain amount of flexibility since I learned to parse a sentence.

I am neither grammarian nor lexicographer. I AM an editor and I have my style preferences and whims even as other editors. Yet, there are some basic things in which I believe and in which all editors, to varying degrees, believe. We all have been reporters, writers and editors long enough to know that if copy is cluttered with basically poor grammar, poor spelling, improper word usage and needless words it is not doing a job for the reader. Feature writing is as demanding in this respect, perhaps moreso, as any field of journalism.

As for your grammar, your spelling and your use of words, remember my suggestion in Chapter Two: Make the dictionary, the thesaurus and Strunk & White's "Elements of Style" your journalistic bibles. You and I are concerned here with the feature story and if you have not absorbed correct grammar and spelling and word definitions sufficiently before now, it is time you started. Failure to do so will mean failure as a feature writer.

I emphasize the elimination of needless words for our present purposes.

For years the trend in journalism has been to "tight writing." By "tight writing" we are not talking about cramming a top story worth display into a few sentences. We are talking about elimination of needless words.

We are talking about use of the ACTIVE verb instead of the PASSIVE verb. We are talking about minimal use of adjectives unless an adjective is hard-hitting descriptively and pertinent to the story.

We are talking about the use of one word to do the work of two or three or four, sometimes even more. And we are talking about ADDING words if the situation can be made clearer to the reader. The whole idea is to make the reader "see" the word picture.

Repeatedly, I scrawl "wordy" across a student's paper. Here's an example. It involved elimination of words, addition of words in certain situations for the sake of clarity, the active verb instead of passive phrasing, virtually the gamut of such problems.

Have you ever met a VIP? ~~If so,~~ what did you experience? ~~Fright, nostalgia or just plain excitement?~~ Did you blush or stutter and say something silly off the top of your head? ~~Whatever you might have done, I'm sure~~ it was a normal reaction. *I know it was normal because I did all those things when I met a "VIP."* ~~Experiencing normal reactions I would like to share my personal episode of meeting a "very important person."~~ *Here's how it went.* Dr. James Webb, administrator of ~~one of our nation's fastest growing departments of~~ the National Aeronautics and Space Administration, was recently a visitor to the university. *Spelling!*

My assignment was to ~~get a personal~~ interview *him* ~~with this dignitary.~~ My first reaction was that of a cool, collected reporter. Let's face it, I didn't have any idea of how important Dr. Webb is. *But* ~~After~~ hours of researching my man in the *libraries* ~~university library and the engineering library, which is located in no woman's land,~~ I started getting my first

What has nostalgia to do with it?

Smoother transition

It isn't interview sional?

other pertinent story pertinent story

[Left margin handwritten notes:] Repetitious — you used the verb start / Inference in bad taste / Of course you were trying / Pertinent only if they had kicked you out / The active verb

~~symptoms of~~ panic. *Yet* I told myself ~~that~~ important
persons ~~people~~ are human ~~too,~~ aren't they? Anyway it was
my job ~~to find Dr. Webb's human streak.~~

I approached several university officials ~~trying~~
to set up ~~a planned~~ *an* interview ~~but was informed of~~
Dr. Webb's *was too* busy ~~schedule and short~~ *this* visit ~~in Columbia~~
too brief[?] ~~before and after his speech. I was politely advised~~ *(They suggested)*
that my only hope of getting close to Webb was to
~~stick to him like his~~ *Shadow* ~~shadow.~~

This ~~didn't sound too unpromising~~ *sounded logical,* but how can
you ~~be a~~ shadow ~~to~~ a man ~~who is~~ surrounded by
dozens of more important shadows than you? Perseverance *I decided, was* ~~is~~ the ~~only~~ answer.

My perseverance lasted through Webb's speech
and up to a special luncheon held for him and the
university deans in the Memorial Student Union.

While listening to ~~Dr. Webb~~ *him* speak, I gained
more insight into his personality, but that ~~still~~ didn't
bring me any closer to my goal.

I was surprised by his *grasp of* ~~dynamic speaking ability~~
~~to~~ a young audience; ~~as~~ I *had* armed myself ~~beforehand~~
with a technological dictionary to help me interpret
the topic ~~he was pursuing. However, I was able to~~

[Lower left margin handwritten notes:] Obviously / Obviously

set my book aside ~~and listen to his words spoken in~~ *He used*

layman's language.

Webb's speech was received by an appreciative

audience, including me. ~~However,~~ the thought ~~was~~

~~still~~ running through my mind, "I've got to meet *Kept*

this man." I waited until the auditorium had cleared

~~and by the time~~ I reached backstage, my quarry had *but when*

~~fled already. My next instinct was~~ to catch him before *disappeared (I decided*

he ~~got involved in the~~ luncheon. *sat down to*

I found the room ~~that was~~ set up for the luncheon

and ~~waited until someone who~~ looked important ~~showed~~ *asked someone who*

~~and then I asked~~ if he had seen Webb. Apparently my

question sounded pertinent because he did answer

~~by saying~~ "He's around."

I knew that he was around but the question was

"Where?" My watch ~~kept an accurate count of~~ the *ticked off*

minutes ~~that were passing~~ as I stood waiting in the

hall outside the luncheon room.

*ok / audition / * / repetitious*

###############

The emphasis in this example is on needless words as indicated by the editing. Yet, it illustrates the occasional need for ADDITIONAL words for the sake of clarity and smoothness. By the way, to answer your question: The reporter finally shook hands with the "dignitary" but did NOT pin him down for the interview.

Here's another example:

In ~~the beginning of~~ *early* September a letter ~~quietly~~

Have you read a noisy letter?

~~found its way into a newspaper office and~~ dropped *was*

on the editor's desk, In ~~truth it fell into the hands~~ *turn* *was given to*

~~of~~ a reporter and ~~he~~ began to ~~conjure up a story.~~ *a story* *unfold.*

I am not defending the lead or approach to this story, which concerned a letter written by a missionary in which she criticized the church in America for its failure to meet the racial issue head-on. The criticism here stresses, again, the needless words.

It boils down to this: You make the active verb do the work and it usually is harder hitting than the words it replaces. When necessary, don't hesitate to ADD words for clarity. You will offset the additions with the subtractions elsewhere in the story.

"The bird ate the worm."

That's the positive or active way to write it. You may substitute another active verb, such as: "The bird swallowed the worm." But if you change the basic format of the sentence, you ADD needless words in the passive voice. For instance: "The worm was eaten by the bird." This is a waste of words and is not as clear as the direct approach with the active verb.

I remember a personal experience. I had covered a legal execution for the first time. I hurried back to the office, hurried out of my coat, hurried to a typewriter, hurriedly beat out what I considered a tremendous lead. Then, I stopped hurrying. I couldn't mesh gears for the second paragraph. Nothing, I mourned, could top that first paragraph:

In the stillness of the midnight hour, at the state prison, John Doe paid with his life in the electric chair for the brutal murder of his wife.

As I sat there staring at the typewriter, the city editor ambled over, read my lead and said: "Son, you can't beat the truth. Get to the point." He pushed me aside and wrote:

John Doe, only 22 years old, died in the state's electric chair at Menard last night for the murder of his wife.

"Now," the city editor said, "remember this: If it's murder, it's brutal and everyone knows it. If it's midnight it is the hour and all is still. And the story is: He's only 22. Gimme the rest of the story, we're running close."

And I did. To this day, I wonder when I would have mentioned the prisoner's age if I had completed the story as I had started it.

And so, preoccupation with adjectives and other needless words can ruin your story.

The list of adjectives is long and most of them aren't necessary. Here are a few of my pet peeves:

(1) She's a PRETTY girl (if she's pretty the feature writer tells the reader about it by weaving her physical description into the story and thereby allowing the reader to judge for himself, something ALL readers love to do.)

(2) The story is VERY good. I tell my students to FORGET the word VERY as they learn to write. If the story is good, it's GOOD. Period!

(3) He is a PROMINENT doctor. If he's PROMINENT, there is no point in telling the reader what he already knows.

(4) The house was TOTALLY demolished. If the house were DEMOLISHED, it was TOTAL.

(5) It was a LARGE crowd. If it qualifies as a CROWD, it's LARGE!

(6) He saw a YOUNG boy. If what he saw was a BOY, the boy is YOUNG!

(7) He was an OLD man of 80. The same situation in reverse.

The list stretches on. If the adjective is pertinent to the story, use it. Mostly, you'll find it needless, repetitious, not hard-hitting enough to warrant its use.

On the point of repetition, another peeve is excessive attribution.

You will find editors divided on this matter. Many still demand repeated establishment of attribution. I also remember the general manager of a newspaper who would call the city desk and say, sarcastically: "From this story about the burglary: I GATHER the source of information was the police. At least, every other sentence has a 'police said' in it."

The point he made was that the information had been attributed to the police in the lead paragraph and he saw no reason to continue attribution the reader undoubtedly recognized.

Once attribution, including quotes, is established, I see no need to repeat attribution UNTIL the SOURCE is changed in identity. A frequent fault of beginners is to compound this repetition. For instance:

"There are a lot of jobs open to women in Columbia," Mrs. Hazel Murdock, president of the Business and Professional Women's Club, SAID. "Holding a job makes women more responsible and interested in civic affairs," SHE SAID.

This is attribution established TWICE in the SAME paragraph. Of course, the last "she said" is needless.

You can save a lot of words, be clearer by crediting the reader with enough sense to know that the attribution continues until you change the identity of source.

In a highly controversial or "delicate" story, you may find attorneys advising constant attribution, So be it. Most of the time it is unnecessary.

Choice of words!

Uncluttered, to-the-point, dramatic words doing the work of many.

This is the responsibility of the feature writer. Just as another responsibility is to mesh his story with the photographs or other art which go with any well-displayed feature story.

Chapter IX

The Cutline

It may surprise you, the beginner in feature writing, to realize that part of your responsibility for the finished, published product is the art — the photographs or drawings which illustrate the well-displayed feature story.

This responsiblity varies according to the publication and the editor for whom you write the story. Publications staffed with their own photographic and arts departments probably will minimize your role in the display. The smaller the publication, the greater is your responsibility.

As the reporter covering the story, though, the publication whose editors do not have YOU write the cutlines (as we arbitrarily shall call them here) is risking embarrassment as well as possible lawsuits. YOU were THERE on the story, YOU probably (and it should be CERTAINLY) worked with the photographer. And the importance of the cutlines under his pictures dictates that YOU write them.

The cutline IS important!

You can beat a cutline to death. And in so doing, you well might beat your newspaper, your magazine or even your television station to death — financially!

For, you see, the cutline (whether you have learned to call it a caption, an underline or "unders") is a condensed feature story.

You dare not toss off the skill in writing cutlines as a minor thing. Some of the greatest feature stories, editorials in journalistic history have been cutlines – one-line cutlines at that. Some of the most costly libel has been committed in cutlines.

What is this thing called a cutline, then?

Simply said, it is the type beneath a picture and it presumably explains the picture. There is more to it than that: It is supposed to COMPLEMENT the picture, to tell the reader what the picture cannot convey. It is NOT supposed to tell the reader what the reader already sees in the picture.

The cutline in general and the function it should serve specifically has been given less attention than any other facet of journalistic training. Too many editors seem to regard the cutline as a sort of Topsy which grows on people naturally. I might add that a tragically good portion of the resultant product attests to that wrong-way attitude.

What most forget is that there has to be a refinement to cutline writing. Its basic purpose is to attract the reader and to accomplish that the cutline has to be interesting reading – interesting and clear and concise.

The test of clarity and conciseness is severest in re-lation to the amount of space allotted the cutline, whether or not there is a tie-in or break-out story with it (and in your case as a feature writer there always is). The variation in the type used for the cutline, how it is set in the composing room is as great as there are publications. You, the cutline writer, must adjust your text to the mechanical demands.

Yet, YOUR responsibility to write a sparkling cutline is NOT mechanical. It calls for you to:

(1) Tell the story the picture CANNOT convey (ordinar-ily identification of persons and locations where pictures are shot).

(2) Tell it well, with a punch.

(3) Pursuant to that goal, to use sound, descriptive words, thereby placing a burden on your skill at choice of words.

(4) Use imagination and originality, geared to fact.

I recall a recent picture of Arnold Palmer at the completion of a swing as a gallery watched him play in the World Series of Golf. The cutlines read:

Incredible! Palmer chips in from 25 feet out for a birdie three on the first hole. When his fans break ranks to shake his hand, he often obliges.

Editorialization? Yes. But then, every golf fan would agree the chip shot was uncommon. The cutlines reported the result of the swing and added the tidbit about his relations with his fans. What the cutlines did NOT say, properly so, was that Palmer was shooting in front of a gallery. The reader could SEE that for himself!

While this was a picture without a related story, the feature writer most frequently must write a cutline for a picture with a related (tie-in or break-out) story. This is the situation wherein cutline writers and editors most commonly bore the reader. They seem obsessed with the need to repeat in the cutlines what has been reported in the story. Their argument usually is that the reader will look only at the picture. I argue that if the cutline is interesting enough, the reader also will take on the story. That inducement is a principal function of the cutline, as well as the picture.

In short, don't pick on a cripple for a lazy cutline; get some meat, some ORIGINAL meat, in the cutline and let the story take care of its own brood of details.

If there is a need for repetition, it usually is found in a quotation taken out of context in the story. An example is a picture illustrating a story about the need for stricter enforcement of the law requiring reports on traffic accidents.

The lead described an accident scene in which a victim lay screaming: "Jesus, come and get me!" And the subsequent report by state troopers that, "Nobody reported that accident, we just happened to stumble across it." The picture was of a smashed car. The cutline read:

> In this man-made coffin, he screamed: "Jesus, come and get me!"

Repetition, yes, but with impact!

There was no repetition of accident details.

The trend in cutline writing is toward brevity. It is geared to recognition of the fact that the reader can see the picture and can read the tie-in story; he needs cutlines to convey what the picture fails to convey and to induce him to read the whole layout.

This is true, too, if a "blurb" is used with a picture layout. The "blurb" is a copy text accompanying the layout and frequently eliminates the necessity for cutlines under each picture. It occurs with picture stories, as the photo people call them. The emphasis here is also on punch and brevity. If cutlines are used under the pictures as well, they should be one-line, boldface affairs emphasizing punch and, again, only complementing the blurb as well as the pictures.

Another problem here is clarity of identification. Your reference in the blurb to each picture must be crystal-clear and orderly.

Certainly the orderly route of identification is mandatory in what we call the sequence layout. This is a series, usually action, of pictures in which the reader almost literally is taken by the hand and led from one picture to another. A series of pictures of action in a football game is a common example. Some editors use the elypsees, or series of dots or periods, at the end of each cutline as a transitional gimmick to the next picture and action. It is an effective layout, IF the cutlines are brief and have impact!

Where brevity and the real test of your skill as a cutline writer come in, however, is found in the one-column, one or two-line cutline.

Of course, the first thing that pops into your mind is the nameline. Simple. Just the guy's name, usually set in boldface. Centered. Well, that's that — let's call it a day and go home. But wait a moment: That ISN'T that!

More than in any other cutline situation, you will be expected most frequently to write this one-column cutline to fit the mood of the picture. The picture could be displayed alone, just a mug shot, or it could be tied in with a story. Whatever the situation, the trend today is to put impact into every cutline. How do you get impact into a nameline situation?

You ADD a line beneath the nameline.

Here are some examples from Time Magazine:

A one-column childhood picture of Walter Slezak, the actor, in an operatic costume to illustrate a story. The line beneath the nameline:

"As 4-year-old Lohengrin"

A picture of Edgar Allen Poe to illustrate a story. The line:

"Death came from something beyond diagnosis"

A picture of Allen Sherman, the comedian-folk singer to illustrate a story. The line:

"Sherman: Ma would be proud"

A picture of Peter Kiewit, illustrating a story of the sale of the Omaha World-Herald to a hometown boy instead of S.I. Newhouse. The line:

"Kiewit: No sale for a Newhouse"

A picture of Joan Crawford and Bette Davis, stars of the film, "Whatever Happened to Baby Jane." The line:

"Joan Crawford and Bette Davis: Sinister Sister Ministering"

You will note that these cutlines feature impact quotes drawn out of context from the tie-in stories. This requires skilled judgment as to which quote fits the mood of the picture. A striking example of this was a picture of a young woman wreathed in a veil with ethereal lighting of her face and background. The line:

"I sometimes think that all the beauty I have is an illusion"

This, of course, was the cutline for a picture more than one column wide, illustrating a tie-in story. This kind of cutline writing is recommended for whatever width of picture illustrating a story.

Whether you're using quotes out of context or an original line, the job requires mental concentration. You can't hide your lack of judgment and originality beneath a wealth of words in a one-liner. You can't bury your lack of imagination and choice of words in 15 or 20 words.

There is still another type of cutline writing where the spotlight is squarely upon the writer. This is the situation wherein the cutline is mortised or cut into the picture itself. As a rule it stands out in bold relief, in contrast to the general color tone of the picture. Your cutline is governed rigidly by the space allotted you in that hole within the picture. The demand for choice of words is severe.

A variation of this type of cutline is the "label" mortised into or pasted onto a picture to identify points in the picture. Ordinarily, this is a simple task but occasionally it calls for some originality. And, let me remind you, a misplaced label can make you and your publication look fairly foolish.

There are numerous traps into which you, the cutline writer, may fall (and many do) and thus embarrass you and your publication. Let's consider some of them. You will note that most of these examples reflect the failure of the writer to credit the reader with common sense and the power of vision.

For instance, there is the picture of a folk singer, armed with a guitar, seated in the midst of teenagers. The cutline reads: "The folk singing of Mary Doe (above)..." ABOVE? Where ELSE could she be? And isn't she the one with a musical instrument and with her mouth open?

Then there is the picture of a man and wife – just two of them. The cutline: "Mrs. Mary Doe (LEFT) smiles at her husband....."

Apparently the writer assumed the reader could not differentiate between man and woman or see that the woman was smiling. This is LAZY and POOR cutline writing!

Consider the picture of two men riding horseback along a road. The cutline: "John Doe and Joe Doe RIDE HORSE–BACK ALONG A ROAD IN VIRGINIA." For some reason, too many cutline writers and their editors simply MUST tell the reader horsemen are on horses.

Or the picture of two men shaking hands. The cutline: "John Doe and Joe Doe SHAKE HANDS as they meet, etc." The reader may not know the identities of the two, but he certainly can SEE that they are shaking hands.

This reminds me of the old standby – the mayor signing a proclamation for "Do-your-business-downtown Day" or some-such. There is the mayor and posed around him are the merchants and all of them are looking straight into the camera and the cutlines are as hackneyed as the posed picture. They read: Mayor Doe reads (or signs) the proclamation while the committee WATCH (or LOOKS ON)..." First, the mayor is NOT seeing or signing anything, he is mugging the camera. And the reader can SEE that the committee is watching or looing on.

Well, we could go on and on. It happens every day in most every publication office in the world.

Fortunately, for every four or five cutlines brushed off in such horrible fashion, there are one or two which reflect the thought put into them. But what worries editors is that there still are and probably always be cutline writers who insist upon writing that Mrs. Doe is on the left of Mr. Doe in a two-person picture.

There still will be cutline writers who will insist on calling every girl in a picture either "pretty" or "striking blonde" or "gorgeous redhead" — when the reader, even with poor reproduction, can see she's virtually an old hag. There still will be writers who insist on writing "shown here" — puttting into print the obvious in pictures instead of using their brains a mite to complement instead of belabor a picture. There still will be writers who will call a man "famous" or "prominent" without pausing to consider that if he really is famous or prominent, the reader doesn't have to be told.

I have mentioned this business about "left to right" when the only persons in the picture are a man and a woman or adult and child. I have seen cutlines for a picture of a man and a dog and the writer tagged the dog as the one on the left.

This all may be amusing and some of it probably is. Except that thinking editors are frightened about libel in cutlines and, to some, the even bigger danger of ridiculing a helpless human being. No thinking editor, nor any thinking reporter or free lance writer, wants to humiliate someone for the sake of humiliation and the amusement it affords the "sick" reader, to use a modern day term. There is a thin line between humor and pathos and ridicule and needless humiliation.

Ridicule of a man or woman or child helpless because of economic disaster or physical or mental incapability cannot be gauged in terms of dollars and cents.

Think of that, you cutline writers, and all of you WILL BE!

Chapter X
Specialized Writing

So now you know something else about feature writing: That a skilled feature writer must be able to write a sparkling, FACTUAL cutline as well as the story which goes with the picture. This may sharpen your awareness of what I said in the beginning: The scope of the feature writer is unlimited.

You will write the newsfeature — the inside story of the humorous or tragic events as they develop in the day's hard news report. You will write the profile — the word picture of a fellow human being. You will write the interpretative — the explanation of the world around you in language the everyday reader can understand and in a format that the everyday reader will enjoy. You will become the refined reporter or researcher; you will master words, the right words in the right places.

As you acquire the experience and the skill to capture the reader, you will be adding to your own education constantly and you will become, in a sense, an educator as you report what you learn. All this, as you follow one feature assignment to another on the way up the professional ladder.

The odds are, of course, that you are ambitious. You want to reach the top in your field and somewhere in this general education you are acquiring as you report and write the odds are, too, you will be intrigued by a particular field. You well may want to specialize in it. It is one way to reach the top.

The demand for skilled feature writers in specialized fields is growing. It sharpens a challenge to you — a chal-

lenge to equip yourself not only with the skill to write but
to KNOW whereof you write!

Government and the arts no longer are the only fields in
which communications media employ specialists. They
steadily are putting more emphasis upon women's news and
the business, labor, religion, science, education and agri-
cultural reports. I refer here to publications of general
circulation. In turn, these fields are emphasizing a better
product in their own publications (commonly called industrial journalism). These are publications of limited circulation aimed at specific fields and markets.

This increased concern by management, whether in
media of general circulation or in industrial journalism,
must rub off on the feature writer it hires. The writer's
responsibility is increased proportionately and how he re-
acts to that challenge is the clue to his success.

The formula is twofold and simple: You must KNOW how
to write, you must KNOW whereof you write!

This is your foundation, wherever you land as a professional. Specialization will not alter the necessity for you to
acquire that general education, to employ all the skill you
may have acquired in each assignment.

You'll note my repeated reference to "general education." This is acquired through general assignments.

There are instances, of course, when a college graduate
begins his professional career as a full-time feature writer
for a publication of general circulation. It depends upon the
individual and his background of education and professional
experience possibly acquired before and during his academic training. Generally, you must expect a period of general
assignment reporting during which your editors will ap-
praise your ability and the degree of polish you still may
need in order to be trusted with major assignments.

This particularly is true of specialization. You cannot

assume that an editor will turn you loose on a major beat or field until he is certain you can handle it. Whether you can — WHEN you can — strictly is up to you. If you have researched the field, if you have made the necessary contacts during your "apprenticeship", if you can WRITE a feature story, your chance of advancement to reporter-interpreter of that field is good.

A man does NOT become a Walter Lippman or David Brinkley or a Frank Luther Mott, a woman does NOT become an Inez Robb or a Sylvia Porter or a Dorothy Roe simply by presenting his or her college diploma to an editor. You must WANT to and be ABLE to write and you must KNOW whereof you write!

This demand is as basic in industrial journalism.

No longer does management toss a company publication to a plumber or sales clerk to edit in his or her spare time. The standards in this field have been upgraded swiftly in the past decade.

Industrial journalism editors know now that their "captive" audiences — the plant workers, the organization fund solicitor, the franchise dealer handling their products — are human beings and while they may tuck the publication under their arms as they leave for home there is no guarantee that they will read it.

They know now that there IS a story behind every routine company handout because they ARE dealing with human beings. And they know now that to find that story, to tell it in a way the captive audience will WANT to read it and understand whatever message there is in it, a trained feature writer must be given the assignment.

They know now that this "captive audience" probably will stretch out in his easy chair and then read the day's news or hear and see it on radio and television, pick up a magazine of general circulation for a story or two, and then glance at the company publication – in that order. That by the time he reaches for the company publication that publication MUST be well-written or he's apt to roll it up and swat flies without further ado.

Industrial journalism has grown up, has become a full-time career for the feature writer who wants to specialize and still have the opportunity to write the gamut of the feature story from newsfeature through the profile to the interpretative. The specialization, of course, lies in the confines of the field the publication represents.

While the rules are the same for you feature writers, basically, there is this difference in the field of industrial journalism: In many situations, the need is for a combination reporter-writer-editor-photographer. Thus, emphasis upon training in copyediting, makeup, photography and typography is indicated as you prepare for such a career.

Essentially, I repeat, the rules are the same. You, the beginner, must realize NOW that whether you work for a publication of general circulation or make industrial journalism your career, the demand for THOROUGH reporting and GOOD writing is standard. Specialization does not change the fundamental requirements, it only accentuates them.

One more thought:

As you go along, you will hear complaints about budgets in both fields. Lack of money restricts imaginative display of stories and pictures, you will hear newspaper, magazine radio and TV editors say. This is more pronounced in the field of industrial journalism.

I call your attention, you beginners, to the argument that there never was a budget so low a publication could not come up with GOOD writing.

I remember a teacher who used to tell her first-grade

pupils: ''I know you're poor, that you can't buy new clothes-
but you always have soap and water and you can keep your-
selves clean!''

Remember this, you future specialists in feature writing: GOOD reporting and GOOD writing are your soap and
water!

Chapter XI

Let's Summarize

As we approach the end of this discussion, I should emphasize a point or two.

The sole objective of this book is to teach you, the scared kid in the college classroom or in the professional field, how to write a feature story. I have not discussed the sale of your story, per se. There is a simple reason for this decision:

You must learn HOW to write a feature story before you can sell it.

When you have learned how, you should be able to sell your story. There are many available references on the art of selling the story. I commend them to you and may your success be great. Here, however, you and I have concentrated upon the business of HOW to write the story. And on this point we shall remain.

I should hope that by now you have a clearer picture of the feature story, that it no longer is an awesome assignment, that you are beginning to enjoy it. I repeat, the feature story could be the most rewarding product of a journalist's effort.

I wonder if you suspect why? I think it is because the feature story is aimed primarily at the man on the street. Your feature story is about him, is written for his enjoyment and his education.

This is true because there are more of him than, say, there are of geniuses. It is true whether you write of war or peace, of famine or abundance, of good or evil – they touch him with the greatest impact. It is the man on the street who makes history, whether by rebellion or subservience, his everyday life or the once-in-a-lifetime flash of brilliance or violence which brings him to public attention.

This is the impact of the feature story, for it touches all men at one time or another.

It is within your future, as beginning feature writers, to make that average man laugh or weep, to show him the difference between apathy and awareness of the world around him. And that is why it is so important that you master the craft you are studying.

It is important that through the use of focus and transition, the proper lead, the proper handling of the body of the article, the proper ending you bring to him all this awareness of life. That you thus bring it to him in a way he enjoys, in a way that he learns something without turning aside because he considers it a chore to understand what you say.

It is important that you add to those fundamental parts of the feature story all the skill you can muster in researching your story, in choosing the right words in the right places once you put down on paper what you have learned through research, through reporting if you please.

The choice of words? Hmm-mm – I recall a television show during which some children were tested on their selection of the right words in the right places.

The moderator asked this boy: "Which is correct: Is he TAKING his lunch or BRINGING his lunch?"

The youngster look at the ceiling, shifted a foot and scratched his head. Finally: "Guess it's whether he's comin' or goin'!"